Secret Gower

Thoughts and images of a magical l

Foreword by Dr. Karl Jenkins OBE B.Mus

Poetry by Diane Norton and photography by Brian Gaylor FRPS. BA(hons)

First published by The Rather Posh Card Company, Swansea. June 2007
Second publication, November 2007

First printed and published in Wales by The Rather Posh Card Company in 2007.

ISBN No. 978-0-9555860-0-4

Design and typesetting by Brian Gaylor.

Large prints of the photographs in this book are available from:- Creative Photo Imaging.
                                                                    Web-site - creativephotoimaging.co.uk

Printed in Swansea by Harcourt Litho Ltd.

For copies of this book contact by EMail --- nortonderek84@hotmail.com

Foreword by Karl Jenkins

Dr. Karl Jenkins, probably the UK's most popular contemporary composer, whose best known works include the 'Adiemus Project' and 'The Armed Man': a mass for peace - has received many prestigious awards, including an OBE in 2005 for his services to British Music.

"Like Diane and Brian, the co-authors of this evocative little book, I was born and raised on the Gower Peninsula, returning to live and compose here after forty years spent in London. As the title suggests, I too have my own secret places that I frequent and the beauty of the peninsula never fails to move me.

It gives me great pleasure, therefore, to commend this book of poems and images of Gower, and would encourage the reader to find their own special places in this Area of Outstanding Natural Beauty".

Dr. Karl Jenkins, OBE B.Mus. F.R.A.M. L.R.A.M. A.R.A.M. F.R.W.C.D.M. F.T.C.C.

Maternal Town

A jumble of streets and houses tumbling down
to the humble seaside town
bumbling along with
its crumbling castle,
chip shops and
churches.

The buffeted bay, bountiful with boats and buoys, bereft now of its trundling train which once rumbled along the seafront laden with fun- seeking trippers eager to sample the joys of Mumbles town.

To stroll along the pier where the lifeboat lurks, catch a glimpse of the ship-warning beam of the lighthouse, visit the Big Apple for buckets and spades, sugar-sweet, nose- tickling candyfloss, toffee apples and pink and white sticks of jaw-aching rock.

Or stumble
mumbling and grumbling
up the steep slopes of the gorse and
heather-clad mount, high above the jewelled
bay of Bracelet, where skylarks soar and robins
sing, to gaze in breathless triumph at the far away hills
and sweep of the sandy shore stretching back to Swansea.

Life's Path

With the light behind me,
I set out along the firm path
above the ever-changing shore
and pause by the well- used seat
which looks forever seawards .
A Christmas wreath lies there still-
"We miss you Mam."

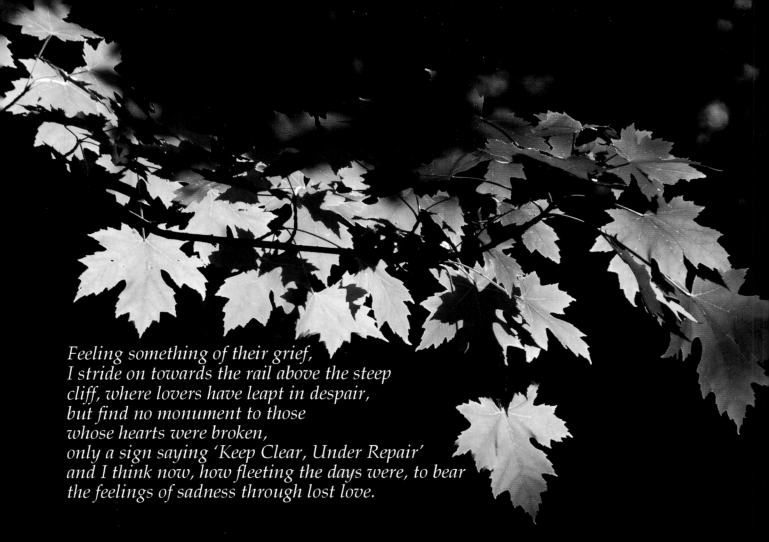

Feeling something of their grief,
I stride on towards the rail above the steep
cliff, where lovers have leapt in despair,
but find no monument to those
whose hearts were broken,
only a sign saying 'Keep Clear, Under Repair'
and I think now, how fleeting the days were, to bear
the feelings of sadness through lost love.

An old man labours up the steep path.
Did he, I wonder, once feel the pain
of love unrequited?
Or did he find another,
easier to claim?
He nods now and smiles,
his only care, perhaps, the strain
on his limbs or the uncharted
miles ahead.

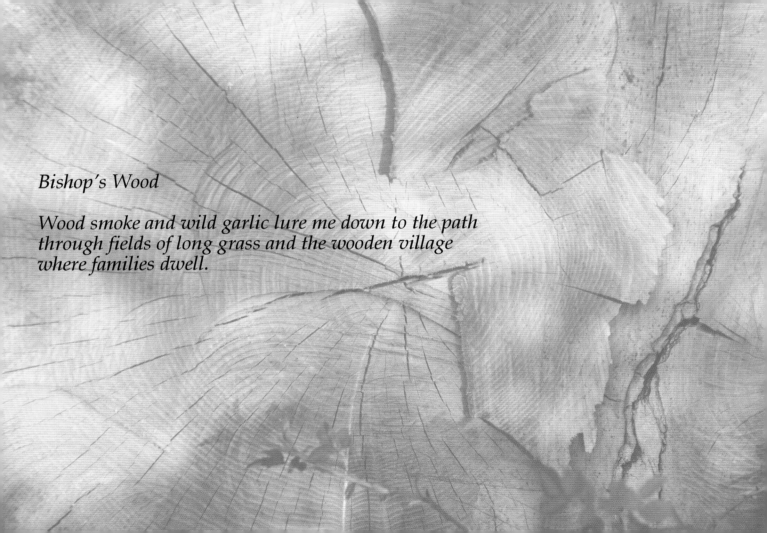

Bishop's Wood

Wood smoke and wild garlic lure me down to the path
through fields of long grass and the wooden village
where families dwell.

Past bikes and trikes children flying kites,
ducks and goats, and muddy slopes
to the ancient wood where men of good will
once drank from the well, their spirits lingering still.

Along the quiet way midst sighing trees,
only the woodpeckers' call breaking the silence
to warn of discord ahead.

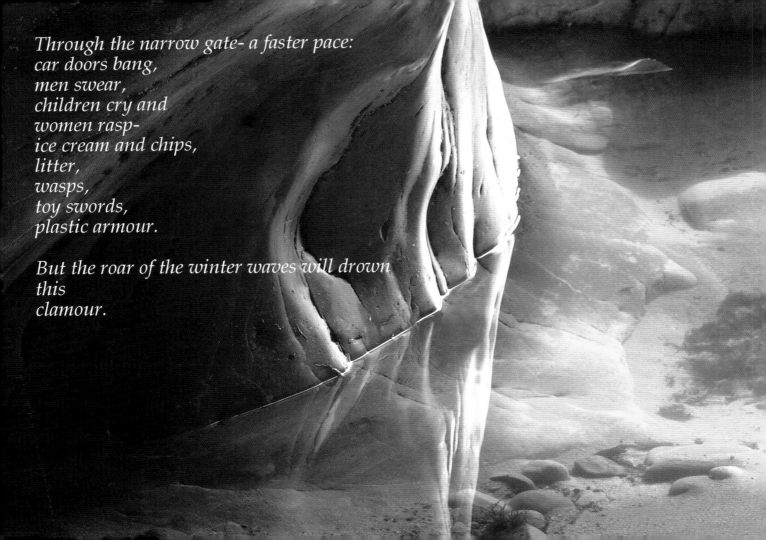

Through the narrow gate- a faster pace:
car doors bang,
men swear,
children cry and
women rasp-
ice cream and chips,
litter,
wasps,
toy swords,
plastic armour.

But the roar of the winter waves will drown
this
clamour.

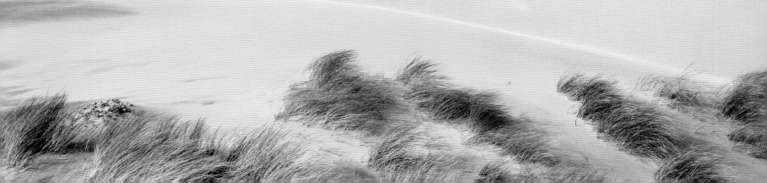

Sea of Life

You enfold me now in your cool embrace
as you race to invade the warm land
not with a shout
but a whisper,
like a hand to a mouth,
leaving no trace
of love upon the sand.
Rising and swelling
like a child in the womb,
bringing new life in your spume,
strewing a seaweed afterbirth
upon the eternal,
maternal shore.

Winter Walk

The sight of the watery sun
on the grey sea,
like a spotlight on a bare stage,
gladdens me.

Fishing boats,
and hills across the still water
form a backdrop to a drama
waiting to begin.

Treading carefully
over tiny brave flowers,
across the sheep-cropped sward
clutching a stone in my pocket,
I walk alone along the familiar path
close to where I was born.

Aeroplanes drone,
seagulls cry,
dogs bark in the distance -
I pause - a momentary qualm-
could the hooded man approaching
with his mobile 'phone
by some mischance
wish me harm?
He passes, still talking,
his dogs in Christmas coats
hurrying ahead.

*I look again for the spotlight
on the sea,
but dark clouds have moved it
away from me.*

Passing By

Scatter my ashes there
where the castle watches over the ancient valley
and the river battles its way
to the sea.

Scatter me
where the gorse glows like sunshine on a mountain top
and the heather covers the hill like carpet
in a rich man's home;
where wild horses roam
and call across the salt dune,
where lovers meet and children play,
where the sea spray
breaks on rocks older than the dale
and pale
people from the towns
warm their bodies in the sun
and run
to the sea.

Scatter me
where I sat with you
and we loved and were young
and old,
where you sheltered me
from the cold
and we laughed
and bore
our children, shoulder high
home from the sandy shore.

Scatter me
where the seagulls cry,
where the sheep graze
and gaze
as we do now in our autumn days
that I too may watch forever,
carefree
in the wind,
while the people, uplifted, pass unaware.

Scatter me there

Trinity Well

In the shadow of the valley, through the gate
beside the Inn, you may tread the pilgrim path
to the ripple of the rill

to where sunlight steals the shade and showers
gold upon the hill and the silence breaks the thunder
of our world.

There you'll find a sacred grove
with a book turned to the page
where Love is etched eternally in stone.

Sand Larks

Billy threw the ball
to Milly,
Milly missed it,
so did Willy;
Billy threw it
willy- nilly;
That was silly
said poor Milly.
Lily said
It's getting chilly,
lets play where it's
not so hilly.
Tilly, riding
on her filly,
galloped off with
silly Billy.

That left Molly
with her dolly
in a supermarket
trolley.
Here comes Polly
with her brolly,
Shall we go and call
for Ollie?
Ollie came with Bert
his collie,
making everyone feel jolly.
Off they went to
gather holly,
which was folly
it
being
mid-
summer.

Channel Chill

A forest of winter-green gorse
at the summit of the Point above the Salt House,
gives no shelter from the wind and icy rain that sweeps
across the sea into every cave and cove and Culver Hole,
full of history and mystery.

Llanmadoc Hill

Today, Llanmadoc Hill is shrouded in a mist
so you can't see the west coast
which is sometimes kissed by sunlight on its shore.
The fog is dense and so the sheep that wander on the heath
are lost from view - unlike the day before.

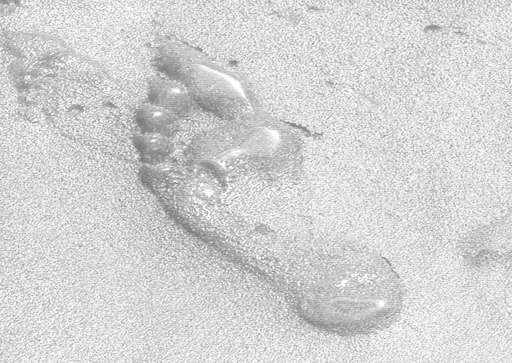

But if you list towards the town
where beds of cockles lie,
and chapel organs rival donkey's bray,
you may perchance just hear the sound of voices lifted high
come drifting, like the mist, across the bay.

Then, if the clinging cloak should rise
unveiling mystic cairns
that look down on the meadows soft and green,
you'll see the tidal river's mouth, then, as you look about,
stretched out before you is a glorious scene:

Of sea and boats and rugged cliffs,
of trees and hills and sky
and cottage homes and daffodils –
or sparrow hawks fly by.

And as you dream, consider this –
that while you're standing still,
the wind may blow and chase the clouds
from old Llanmadoc Hill.

Corner House Farm

Do come, they'd say,
the weather should be fine
and we shall dine
with friends.

So we would race,
at such a pace,
down the grey
motorway,
towards the cottage
by the sea,
where an open door
and G.& T
ready to pour-
and such a fuss
awaited us!

Then the talks
and the walks
down the timeless valley
to the V-shaped beach —
out of reach
of the crazy world —
each shallow cove
with its own grove
of rocks,
giving a sense
of a garden
with a fence.

Later, there'd be wining
and dining,
and singing -
the house ringing
with stories
of past glories.
Such pleasure,
beyond measure;
memories to treasure.

Forever.

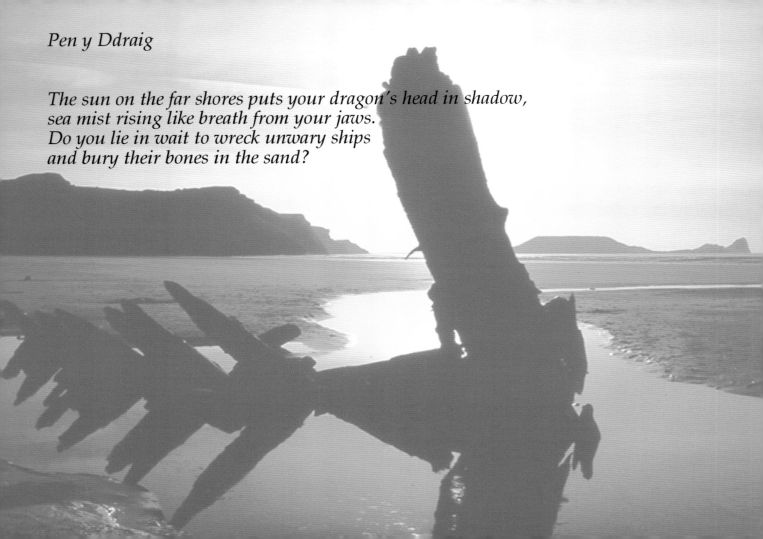

Pen y Ddraig

The sun on the far shores puts your dragon's head in shadow,
sea mist rising like breath from your jaws.
Do you lie in wait to wreck unwary ships
and bury their bones in the sand?

What secrets hide beneath the waves
that break against your sides,
while legions march along your back
to race incoming tides?

The tragedies strewn on the rocks
that gather round your feet
must make your burden heavy
as you guard us, while we sleep.

We ponder your devotion to our land
and bow to your imposing majesty,
but wonder if an aeon hence from now
your presence will be just a memory.

Diane Norton *was born and bred in Gower. She attended junior school at Three Crosses and then secondary school at Penclawdd. When she was twenty-eight she moved to Australia with her husband and two children, where she enjoyed a successful, if brief, career in the professional theatre.*
She eventually returned to Britain and lived and worked for many years in the Midlands, maintaining a keen interest in the theatre and the arts generally, visiting Wales whenever possible.

In 2002, she returned to live, permanently, in her beloved Gower, walking and thinking around its coastal and inland paths. This is her first book of poetry.

Brian Gaylor, *the Swansea photographer, is well known for his stunning landscapes. His love of Gower's glorious scenery is graphically illustrated in this unique book. The photographs portray a sense of tranquillity, harmony and wonder; it is a world of secret corners and undiscovered vantage points.*

Although all the photographic images in this book are of the Gower Peninsula, they have been used to reflect the mood of the poems, rather than to illustrate specific locations.